SandCastle 3

Good Manners

Excuse Me

Kelly Doudna

ABDO
Publishing Company

Published by SandCastle™, an imprint of ABDO Publishing Company, 4940 Viking Drive, Edina, Minnesota 55435.

Cover and interior photo credits: Comstock, Digital Stock, PhotoDisc, Stock Market

Library of Congress Cataloging-in-Publication Data

Doudna, Kelly, 1963-
  Excuse me / Kelly Doudna.
    p. cm. -- (Good manners)
  Includes index.
  ISBN 1-57765-574-5
    1. Courtesy--Juvenile literature. 2. Children--Conduct of life. 3. Etiquette. [1. Etiquette.] I. Title.

BJ1533.C9 D68 2001
395.1'22--dc21

2001022004

The SandCastle concept, content, and reading method have been reviewed and approved by a national advisory board including literacy specialists, librarians, elementary school teachers, early childhood education professionals, and parents.

Let Us Know

After reading the book, SandCastle would like you to tell us your stories about reading. What is your favorite page? Was there something hard that you needed help with? Share the ups and downs of learning to read. We want to hear from you! To get posted on the ABDO Publishing Company Web site, send us email at:

sandcastle@abdopub.com

About SandCastle™

Nonfiction books for the beginning reader

- Basic concepts of phonics are incorporated with integrated language methods of reading instruction. Most words are short, and phrases, letter sounds, and word sounds are repeated.

- Readability is determined by the number of words in each sentence, the number of characters in each word, and word lists based on curriculum frameworks.

- Full-color photography reinforces word meanings and concepts.

- "Words I Can Read" list at the end of each book teaches basic elements of grammar, helps the reader recognize the words in the text, and builds vocabulary.

- Reading levels are indicated by the number of flags on the castle.

Look for more SandCastle books in these three reading levels:

Level 1 (one flag)	Level 2 (two flags)	Level 3 (three flags)

Grades Pre-K to K	**Grades K to 1**	**Grades 1 to 2**
5 or fewer words per page	5 to 10 words per page	10 to 15 words per page

We say "excuse me" if we have done something that is not polite.

We say "excuse me" when someone is in our way or we are in theirs.

We say "excuse me" to be noticed.

This shows that we have good manners.

Emma is eating breakfast.

Her dad says, "Excuse me. Would you like anything else?"

Lee is selling lemonade.

She says, "**Excuse me.**
Would you like to buy
a glass?"

Trevor has trouble with math.

He asks his teacher, "Excuse me. Would you help me?"

Sumi has found the correct spot.

She says, "Excuse me. I know the right answer."

Mr. Smith says, "Excuse me. I wish you would speak more softly in the library."

Juan would like to know what Wade is reading.

What should he say?

Words I Can Read

Nouns

A noun is a person, place, or thing

answer (AN-sur) p. 17
breakfast (BREK-fuhst) p. 11
dad (DAD) p. 11
glass (GLASS) p. 13

lemonade (lem-uh-NADE) p. 13
library (LYE-brer-ee) p. 19
math (MATH) p. 15
spot (SPOT) p. 17

teacher (TEECH-ur) p. 15
trouble (TRUH-buhl) p. 15
way (WAY) p. 7

Proper Nouns

A proper noun is the name of a person, place, or thing

Emma (EM-uh) p. 11
Juan (HWON) p. 21
Lee (LEE) p. 13

Mr. Smith (MISS-tur SMITH) p. 19
Sumi (SOOM-ee) p. 17

Trevor (TREV-ur) p. 15
Wade (WADE) p. 21

Plural Nouns

A plural noun is more than one person, place, or thing

manners (MAN-urz) p. 9

Pronouns

A pronoun is a word that replaces a noun

anything (EN-ee-thing) p. 11
he (HEE) pp. 15, 21
I (EYE) pp. 17, 19
me (MEE) pp. 5, 7, 9, 11, 13, 15, 17, 19

she (SHEE) pp. 13, 17
someone (SUHM-wuhn) p. 7
something (SUHM-thing) p. 5
theirs (THAIRZ) p. 7

this (THISS) p. 9
we (WEE) pp. 5, 7
what (WUHT) p. 21
you (YOO) pp. 11, 13, 15, 19

22

Verbs

A verb is an action or being word

are (AR) p. 7

asks (ASKSS) p. 15

be (BEE) p. 9

buy (BYE) p. 13

done (DUHN) p. 5

eating (EET-ing) p. 11

excuse (ek-SKYOOZ)
pp. 5, 7, 9, 11, 13, 15,
17, 19

found (FOUND) p. 17

has (HAZ) pp. 15, 17

have (HAV) pp. 5, 9

help (HELP) p. 15

is (IZ) pp. 5, 7, 11, 13, 21

know (NOH) pp. 17, 21

like (LIKE) pp. 11, 13, 21

noticed (NOH-tist) p. 9

reading (REED-ing) p. 21

say (SAY) pp. 5, 7, 9, 21

says (SEZ)
pp. 11, 13, 17, 19

selling (SEL-ing) p. 13

should (SHUD) p. 21

shows (SHOHZ) p. 9

speak (SPEEK) p. 19

wish (WISH) p. 19

would (WUD)
pp. 11, 13, 15, 19, 21

Adjectives

An adjective describes something

correct (kuh-REKT) p. 17

else (ELSS) p. 11

good (GUD) p. 9

her (HUR) p. 11

his (HIZ) p. 15

our (OUR) p. 7

polite (puh-LITE) p. 5

right (RITE) p. 17

Adverbs

An adverb tells how, when, or where
something happens

else (ELSS) p. 11

more (MOR) p. 19

softly (SAWFT-lee) p. 19

Glossary

breakfast – the first meal of the day.

lemonade – a drink made from lemon juice, water, and sugar.

library – a place where books, magazines, newspapers, records, and videos are kept for reading or borrowing.

manners – polite behavior.